Primary Sources of the Civil Rights Movement

Ida B. Wells-Barnett and the Crusade against Lynching

Alison Morretta

Cavendish Square

New York

Published in 2017 by Cavendish Square Publishing, LLC
243 5th Avenue, Suite 136, New York, NY 10016

Library of Congress Cataloging-in-Publication Data

Names: Morretta, Alison, author.
Title: Ida B. Wells-Barnett and the crusade against lynching / Alison Morretta.
Description: New York : Cavendish Square Publishing, [2017] | Series: Primary sources of the Civil Rights Movement | Includes bibliographical references and index.
Identifiers: LCCN 2015050693 (print) | LCCN 2016006291 (ebook) | ISBN 9781502618740 (library bound) | ISBN 9781502618757 (ebook)
Subjects: LCSH: Wells-Barnett, Ida B. | African American women--Biography. | African American women civil rights workers--Biography. | African American women social reformers--Biography. | Lynching--United States--History. | United States--Race relations--History.
Classification: LCC E185.97.W55 M67 2017 (print) | LCC E185.97.W55 (ebook) | DDC 323.092--dc23
LC record available at http://lccn.loc.gov/2015050693

Editorial Director: David McNamara
Editor: Fletcher Doyle
Copy Editor: Nathan Heidelberger
Art Director: Jeffrey Talbot
Designer: Amy Greenan
Production Assistant: Karol Szymczuk
Photo Research: J8 Media

CONTENTS

INTRODUCTION • 4
The Price of Freedom

CHAPTER ONE • 7
Life Becomes a Reality

CHAPTER TWO • 18
To Tell the Truth Freely

CHAPTER THREE • 32
A Crusader for Justice

CHAPTER FOUR • 44
Unsung Hero

Chronology • 54

Glossary • 56

Further Information • 58

Bibliography • 60

Index • 62

About the Author • 64

The Price of Freedom

O n December 6, 1865, slavery in the United States officially came to an end with the ratification of the Thirteenth Amendment to the Constitution. Even though the slaves were free, they still did not have the same rights and protections as white people. After the war, the government's first priority was to bring the former rebel states back into the Union. Republicans in Congress and President Andrew Johnson disagreed on how to do this. This postwar reform period, known as Reconstruction, lasted from 1865 to 1877 and had two stages: Presidential Reconstruction (1865–1867) and Radical Reconstruction (1867–1877).

President Johnson wanted to bring the South back into the Union as quickly as possible and had very lenient requirements for the rebel states to be accepted: they must uphold the Thirteenth Amendment abolishing slavery, swear loyalty to the Union, and pay their war debts. The rights of ex-slaves were of no importance to him. He granted presidential pardons to many ex-Confederate leaders and

The southern black codes imposed penalties on free blacks who broke labor contracts. They could be sold to work off their debt, as depicted in this 1867 illustration.

returned confiscated land to former slaveholders. This allowed those who had been in power before the war to regain control over their state governments, and they immediately began to pass discriminatory laws known as **black codes**. These laws restricted the freedom of ex-slaves, essentially returning them to their former slave status with one important exception—since freedmen were no longer the property of white Southerners, the former slave owners had no reason to protect the freedmen from physical harm.

The Radical Republicans in Congress, who wanted to protect the rights of black Americans and usher in a new way of life in the South, were outraged by the president's lenient policies. Johnson vetoed all the bills passed in Congress meant to help former slaves, but the Radical Republicans were able to pass laws over the president's objections. Radical Reconstruction saw the passage of several acts granting civil rights to black Americans, as well as the Reconstruction Act of 1867, which put the South under military rule. The act

This 1874 cartoon from *Harper's Weekly* shows black voters being disenfranchised at the polls by a group of white supremacists.

changed the conditions for reentry into the Union: Confederate states were required to ratify the Fourteenth Amendment, which gave full citizenship rights to black Americans; adopt new state constitutions that prohibited ex-Confederates from holding office; and guarantee black men's right to vote.

Under Radical Reconstruction, black Southerners had hope that things would improve, but Southern whites would not give up power without a fight. Racial violence increased in the South, often in the form of **lynchings**. White mobs were permitted to take the law into their own hands, and any black American accused of a crime could be denied his or her legal right to a trial and publicly executed. Prejudice did not end with slavery, and Southerners were willing to use violence to maintain white supremacy.

It was into this turbulent environment that Ida B. Wells was born. The future journalist and activist grew up in the Deep South, and even as a child, she could see there was no justice for her race. Wells refused to let her race or her gender keep her from speaking out against the injustices she witnessed. Despite the dangers she faced, Wells made it her life's work to fight for the rights and protections she knew black Americans deserved, and despite all odds, she became a crusader for justice.

Life Becomes a Reality

I da Bell Wells was born a slave in Holly Springs, Mississippi, on July 16, 1862, nearly three years before the end of the Civil War. Though she had no experience with slavery, Ida learned from the experiences of her parents, Jim Wells and Lizzie Warrenton. Young Ida also learned that being free did not mean being equal. She experienced the discrimination and violence that plagued black Americans in the South, and her experiences as a young woman had a strong influence on the course her life would take.

Early Memories

Like so many slaves, Jim Wells was the son of his white master. When Jim was eighteen, he was apprenticed to a builder and contractor in Holly Springs named Spires Boling. In Holly Springs, Jim met Lizzie, a slave cook in Boling's kitchen. Although they could not legally marry, they lived

A present-day view of the downtown area of Holly Springs, Mississippi, where Wells was born and lived as a child.

together and started a family. Ida was the first of many children, although only five survived to adulthood.

One of Wells's first memories was overhearing a conversation between her father and his mother in which Jim recounted how Miss Polly (Jim's father's wife) had his mother whipped after Jim's master/father died. Jim told his mother, "I guess it is all right for you to take care of [Miss Polly] and forgive her for what she did to you, but she could have starved to death if I'd had my say-so." In Wells's autobiography, *Crusade for Justice*, she wrote: "I have never forgotten those words. Since I have grown old enough to understand I cannot help but feel what an insight into slavery they gave."

The perceptive young Ida was also aware of the danger that lurked outside their happy home. As a freedman in the South during Radical Reconstruction, Jim Wells was very politically active, but by attending political meetings and voting, he was risking his life. As soon as ex-slaves were given political power, white supremacists began to **disenfranchise** them. They instituted **poll taxes** and **literacy tests** designed to weed out poor, uneducated black voters, and often resorted to intimidation and violence.

This 1867 illustration shows hooded members of the Ku Klux Klan about to lynch President Abraham Lincoln. Lincoln was assassinated in 1865, just days after the end of the Civil War.

The Ku Klux Klan (KKK) was formed during Reconstruction as a way to stop black men (and white Republicans) from voting and to keep white Southern Democrats in power. Wells remembered reading the newspaper to her father as a young girl: "I heard the words Ku Klux Klan long before I knew what they meant," she recalled. "I knew dimly that it meant something fearful, by the anxious way my mother walked the floor at night when my father was out to a political meeting." Wells learned early that it was a dangerous thing for black people to exercise their legal rights.

The Importance of Education

The Freedmen's Bureau was a federal agency created to aid ex-slaves during Reconstruction. Among other services, the

Rust College in Holly Springs, Mississippi, was established by the Freedmen's Bureau to educate former slaves. Wells, her siblings, and her mother all attended classes at Rust (then called Shaw University).

bureau established schools throughout the South to educate former slaves. One such school was Rust College in Holly Springs, where Wells, her mother, and her siblings attended classes. Lizzie attended long enough to be able to read the Bible. She was very religious and attended Sunday school with her children every week. As far as Lizzie's children were concerned, their "job was to go to school and learn all [they] could."

While the children attended school, Jim Wells provided for the family. He owned his own carpentry business and the Wells family home. He was a **race man**—a member of the black community active in business as well as social and political groups dedicated to the uplift of the race. The Wells family was financially independent, which was rare in the South, where many children had to forgo education in order to work to help the family. This was not so for Ida Wells, and with her parents as role models, she learned the importance of education, religion, and social consciousness.

A Childhood Cut Short

In the summer of 1878, a **yellow fever** epidemic struck Memphis, Tennessee, and spread to Holly Springs. Both Jim and Lizzie Wells (and Ida's infant brother Stanley) died from the disease. Ida was visiting her grandparents' farm and was unaware that the disease had even reached her hometown when she received a letter informing her that her parents were dead. It was at this moment, she recalls, that "life became a reality."

Wells rushed home to be with her siblings and found that a group of her father's friends planned to split up the family. Sixteen-year-old Wells put her foot down, refusing to allow the adults to break her family apart. She told them, "it would make my father and mother turn over in their graves to know their children had been scattered." Thus, "after being a happy, lighthearted schoolgirl [Wells] suddenly found [herself] at the head of a family."

This brave decision came with unexpected consequences. There was a doctor in town who was holding money for her family, and when Wells went to get it from him, the townspeople began to spread rumors that young Ida "had been heard asking white men for money" and implied that was the reason she wanted to stay at home alone with her siblings. Ida wrote that she had never "suffered such a shock as I did when I heard this misconstruction that had been placed upon my determination to keep my brothers and sisters together."

Wells's virtue and reputation were attacked, and she was introduced to one of the terrible stereotypes that plagued black women: that they were promiscuous and did not have the same virtue that white women had. The simple act of publicly taking money from a white man was enough to make people believe that Wells, a child of sixteen, was in an inappropriate relationship with an adult man.

Wells's grandmother came to Holly Springs to help care for the children (and protect Ida's reputation) while Ida worked as a teacher at a rural school 6 miles (9.6 kilometers) outside Holly Springs. It was too far to travel every day (the only transportation was by mule), so she stayed the week in the country and came home on weekends to help out. She was not making enough money to support the family, and the nonstop work and travel were taking a toll on her, so when her aunt Fannie invited her (and her two youngest siblings, Annie and Lily) to come live with her in Memphis, she accepted. Ida was forced to break up the family, but at least she knew her two brothers, James and George, and her other sister, Eugenia, would be cared for by her aunt Belle and not sent to live with strangers.

The Railroad Lawsuit

Wells moved to Memphis in 1881 and got a job at a school 10 miles (16.1 km) outside the city. In Memphis, she was able to take the train to and from work. Tennessee had just passed its first **Jim Crow law** allowing segregation on the railroads. There were supposed to be separate "colored" cars for first-class black passengers, equal in quality to the first-class cars for whites, but this was rarely the case. The law was not regularly enforced until 1883, when the Supreme Court overturned the Civil Rights Act of 1875, legalizing segregation in public spaces.

Exclusion from a first-class car was especially harmful to black women. Trains had separate ladies' cars, which were more comfortable and kept women isolated from single men while they were traveling alone. Since a woman's reputation was of the utmost importance, the exclusion of black women from the ladies' car was particularly damaging.

White women sit in a ladies' train car, circa 1901. Jim Crow laws legally segregated the races on public transportation for decades after the end of the Civil War.

On September 15, 1883, Wells boarded the train and sat in the ladies' car with her first-class ticket. When the conductor came to check tickets, he told her that she had to leave and go to the smokers' car (a second-class car filled with single men). Wells believed that she deserved the same protection and respect given to white women and refused to leave. The conductor tried to drag her out, but she would not go without a fight. She bit his hand and held on tight to the seat, but he got two other men to help him remove her. While this was happening, the white people in the car encouraged them, and "some of them even stood on the seats

This portrait of Ida B. Wells was taken in the 1890s, shortly after her journalism career took off and she became known as "Iola, Princess of the Press."

so they could get a good view and continued applauding the conductor for his brave stand."

Wells got off the train instead of going to the smoker's car, and when she returned to Memphis, she was determined to sue the railroad company. She hired a black attorney, Thomas F. Cassels, but she fired him when she learned that he had been paid off by the railroad to throw her case. She was incredibly disappointed that a black community leader and professional would not stand up for his own race, but she ended up initially winning her lawsuit with the help of white attorney James M. Greer and was awarded $300 in damages.

This experience launched Wells's journalism career. In 1884, she wrote her first article: a report of her lawsuit

Breaking Boundaries

Wells was a controversial figure from the start. She did not write about the traditional subjects reserved for female writers (domestic tasks, child rearing, etc.); instead, she took on issues like racial discrimination and politics, which were considered to be outside the scope of a woman's understanding. Wells was not afraid to criticize the men in power, as she showed in one of her early pieces for the *Living Way*.

In "Functions of Leadership," Wells voiced her displeasure with the black elites who did not use their position in society to help the less fortunate members of the black community. She believed it was the responsibility of those with wealth and status to aid others, and she criticized those who thought leading by example was enough:

> All of us can not be millionaires, orators, lawyers, doctors; what then must become of the mediocrity, the middle and lower classes ... What material benefit is a "leader" if he does not, to some extent, devote his time, talent and wealth to the alleviation of the poverty and misery, and elevation of his people?

published in the black newspaper the *Living Way*. Despite Wells's initial victory, the Tennessee Supreme Court overturned the verdict in 1887. Wells recorded her disappointment in the diary she kept during her years in Memphis:

> I had hoped such great things from my suit for my people ... I have firmly believed all along that the law was on our side and would, when we appealed to it, give us justice. I feel shorn of that belief and utterly discouraged, and just now if it were possible would gather my race in my arms and fly far away with them.

Even though she lost her suit against the railroad, Wells discovered her true passion. She continued teaching for the money, but journalism gave a voice to a fearless woman who was not afraid to speak out.

Iola, Princess of the Press

After her railroad article was published, Wells continued to write a weekly unpaid column for the *Living Way*. She signed her articles with the **pseudonym** "Iola" and wrote about racial issues. While Wells was not the first woman to enter the public sphere, for a black woman to do so in the South was almost unheard of. In **Victorian-era** America, women were expected to keep to the private sphere of the home and only concern themselves with domestic things; the public sphere, which included social and political issues, was reserved for men.

In 1886, Wells joined the Memphis Lyceum literary society—a social club which held debates and book discussions—and she was asked to edit the club newspaper, the *Evening Star*. Wells's first paid writing job, at the sum of $1 a week, was for the *American Baptist*, edited by

William J. Simmons. Simmons was also the president of the National Negro Press Association, and he sent Wells to a press convention in Louisville, Kentucky, where she was the first woman representative.

Wells's articles were reprinted in black papers across the country, and by the late 1880s, she was given the nickname "Iola, Princess of the Press." She attended the 1889 Afro-American Press Convention in Washington, DC, where she met influential black leaders Frederick Douglass and T. Thomas Fortune, both of whom would play important roles in her life and career. Fortune, editor of the *New York Age*, wrote that Wells "[wrote] as easily as any man in newspaper work. If Iola were a man she would be a humming independent in politics. She has plenty of nerve and is as sharp as a steel trap." What Fortune and others did not know was that Wells would never allow her gender to stop her from doing anything a man could do.

T. Thomas Fortune, editor of the influential black paper the *New York Age*, was a great supporter of Wells's work.

To Tell the Truth Freely

W ells's growing popularity was due to the fact that she wrote for the masses, not the black elite. As a teacher in the rural South, Wells came into contact with many uneducated former slaves who "needed guidance in everyday life" and were not getting it from the church and community leaders. Discussing her *Living Way* articles, she wrote that she knew from experience that "the people who had little or no school training should have something coming into their homes weekly which dealt with their problems in a simple, helpful way." With this in mind, Wells said she wrote her articles "in a plain, common-sense way on the things which concerned our people. Knowing that their education was limited, [she] never used a word of two syllables where one would serve the purpose."

An Equal Partner

No longer content to write for small sums, in 1889 Wells became the editor of a Memphis paper, the *Free Speech*

This 1866 engraving shows white teachers educating black students in a Richmond, Virginia, Freedmen's Bureau school. During Reconstruction, teachers were almost all northern white women, but their black students (like Wells) would go on to become teachers themselves.

and Headlight. The paper was owned by Reverend Taylor Nightingale and J. L. Fleming, and Wells "refused to come in except as equal with themselves." She bought a one-third interest in the paper and made some changes: She shortened the title to *Free Speech* and started printing it on pink paper. She did this because people who could not read would buy a copy for someone to read to them, but salesmen often took advantage of them and sold them the wrong paper. In pink, the *Free Speech* stood out from all the others, and Wells made sure that all members of the black community, regardless of education, had access to it.

Wells was still teaching during her early days at the *Free Speech*, but her 1891 article criticizing the Memphis school system got her fired. She wrote about how much worse the conditions were for black schoolchildren compared with those for whites. The controversy started when she made the accusation that some of the unqualified teachers "had little to recommend them save an illicit friendship with members of the school board." She knew that this was a dangerous statement to publish, and she originally asked that Reverend Nightingale sign the editorial. When he refused, she published it anyway and lost her job in the Memphis city school system.

Despite the consequences, Wells did not regret it because she "thought it was right to strike a blow against a glaring evil." She was, however, disappointed that no one stood up for her. She wrote, "Up to that time I had felt that any fight made in the interest of the race would have its support. I learned then that I could not count on that."

The Curve Lynchings

In March 1892, Wells's life changed forever when three black men—Thomas Moss, Calvin McDowell, and Will Stewart—were murdered by a white mob in an area outside Memphis known as the Curve. Moss was Wells's close friend and part owner of the People's Grocery, a black-owned business in competition with a white-owned store across the street; McDowell and Stewart worked at the store.

The white storeowner, William Barrett, had long been determined to eliminate his competition. After an incident of racial violence in the Curve, Barrett started rumors that the People's Grocery men had tried to start a race riot and attempted to have his competition arrested. When this failed, he spread the rumor that a white mob was going to attack the People's Grocery. The black community could not get help from the Memphis police because the Curve was outside the city borders. With no other options to protect themselves and their business, the men of the People's Grocery armed themselves and guarded the store.

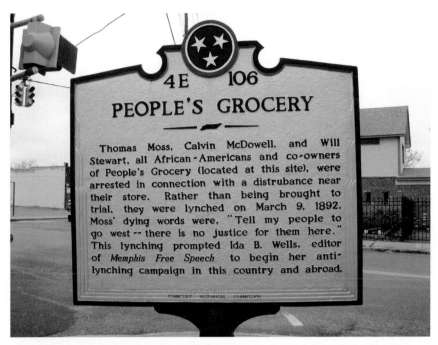

This marker stands at the corner of Walker Avenue and Mississippi Boulevard in Memphis, Tennessee, where the black-owned People's Grocery was once located. It commemorates the Curve lynchings that prompted Wells to start her crusade.

With the help of the local sheriff, Barrett had a group of white citizens deputized (made temporary law officers), and on the night of March 5, the group of white men came to the People's Grocery. None of the deputies were in uniform, and the men in the People's Grocery mistook them for the rumored mob. A gunfight broke out in which three of the deputies were injured.

On Sunday morning, the white newspapers in Memphis published false facts about the incident, mischaracterizing the People's Grocery as "a low dive" where "drinking and gambling were carried on" and saying the black-owned business was "a resort of thieves and thugs." The police raided black homes and dragged many men to the jail with no real evidence of their involvement. Moss, McDowell, and Stewart were arrested and accused of being the ringleaders of the attack. For days

SCENES IN MEMPHIS, TENNESSEE, DURING THE RIOT—BURNING A FREEDMEN'S SCHOOL-HOUSE

[Sketched by A. R. W.]

This illustration from *Harper's Weekly* shows the burning of a Freedmen's Bureau schoolhouse during the Memphis race riot of 1866. There was a history of racial violence in Memphis long before the Curve lynchings.

after the arrests, white men gathered at the jail (they were even permitted to enter to look at the men), and they openly discussed lynching on the streets. The Memphis papers fueled the racial tension by publishing false accounts of events.

Fearing for the safety of the prisoners, the Tennessee Rifles (a black militia unit) stood guard at the jail for days, until the papers reported that the injured men would recover. The Rifles believed that the men were out of danger and left, but in the early morning hours of March 9, a white mob dragged the three men from their jail cells, took them outside the city by railroad, and shot them to death. The Memphis papers reported the lynchings in gory detail, including Moss's last words: "Tell my people to go West—there is no justice for them here."

Fearing retribution, the mob went to a local judge, who told the sheriff to "take a hundred men" to the Curve and "shoot down on sight any Negro who appears to be making trouble." The black community hid in their homes, but the lynch mob was not satisfied. They looted and destroyed the People's Grocery, eliminating Barrett's competition once and for all.

Seeking the Truth

Wells was in Natchez, Mississippi, gathering subscriptions for her paper when she heard the tragic news. The lynching of her friend and the others devastated Wells, but it also made her angry. This was not the first lynching she had heard of, but the reports of the lynchings she had heard were always tied to accusations of sexual assault. Wells had previously believed that, while vigilante justice was not necessarily right, sexual assault was such a horrible crime that lynching was almost justified.

With Moss and the other men, it was different. She knew that Moss was an upstanding member of the community—a kind, family man who worked hard to get ahead. Additionally, there were no accusations of sexual assault at the Curve.

JOHN HARTFIELD WILL BE
LYNCHED BY ELLISVILLE MOB
AT 5 O'CLOCK THIS AFTERNOON

Governor Bilbo Says He Is Powerless to Prevent It—
Thousands of People Are Flocking Into Ellisville to
Attend the Event—Sheriff and Authorities Are Power-
less to Prevent It.

The NAACP compiled newspaper clippings of lynching announcements as a fundraising measure. The bottom of the NAACP flyer (top image) reads, "What Will You Do To Help Stop This?"

This abandoned house is located in Clearview, Oklahoma, one of the historically black towns founded during the settlement of the Oklahoma Territory in the late 1800s.

"Go West"

In the first article Wells wrote after the Curve lynchings, she honored Thomas Moss's final words by urging her readers to save their money and leave town. When Wells spoke, black Memphis listened, and people began to leave for the Oklahoma Territory, where there were several all-black settlements. The exodus of black Memphians hurt the city's white-owned businesses, and papers began to publish negative things about the conditions in Oklahoma. Wells continued to urge people to leave, but she wanted them to have correct information before deciding where to go. She traveled to Oklahoma to investigate and published the unbiased facts so that people could make an informed decision.

By early May, Memphis had lost around 20 percent of its black population. The white-owned City Railway Company was so desperate that two men came to Wells's office and asked her to help get black people riding the trolley cars again. She refused, telling them that "the colored people feel that every white man in Memphis … is as guilty as those who fired the guns … and they want to get away from this town."

These murders "opened [her] eyes to what lynching really was. An excuse to get rid of Negroes who are acquiring wealth and property and thus keep the race terrorized." Wells thus began her career as an investigative journalist determined to publish the facts about every lynching she heard about.

Wells started her investigative work in 1892—the year that had the highest recorded number of reported lynchings in history, more than two hundred. She traveled throughout the South to locations of reported lynchings, interviewing people to learn the truth of the alleged crimes. In many cases, she found that what had been reported in the papers was false. Wells discovered that black men lynched for alleged murders were often scapegoats for white criminals (some of whom disguised themselves in **blackface**). She uncovered false accounts of sexual assault that were actually **consensual relationships**. She even learned that black men could be lynched for something as simple as being disrespectful to a white person.

She also learned the disturbing fact that white papers often supported lynchings and encouraged readers to attend these murders before they happened. There was evidence that government officials not only failed to protect prisoners but actively helped the mobs. Wells wanted to bring these things to light in the *Free Speech*, and she did so despite the risk. She knew that publishing these facts might bring lynch mobs to her door, and she kept a pistol in her office. After the Curve lynchings, she "expected some cowardly retaliation" and she was willing to "die fighting against injustice."

Exile

Her concerns were proven valid when, on May 21, 1892, Wells published the *Free Speech* editorial that changed her life. Among other horrible injustices, it had become clear to her that most of the accusations of sexual assault were lies and cover-ups. She aimed to expose this truth in her daring editorial:

> Nobody ... believes the old thread-bare lie that Negro men rape white women. If Southern white men are not careful they will over-reach themselves and a conclusion will be reached which will be very damaging to the moral reputation of their women.

Wells was saying what many people knew but did not discuss: that black men and white women had consensual relationships. Not only did **anti-miscegenation laws** make interracial relationships a crime (miscegenation is sexual relations or marriage between people of different races), any white woman in a relationship with a black man was considered unvirtuous; her reputation would be ruined. She would bring shame on her family—especially the male relatives, who were supposed to protect her. With so much at stake, white women who were discovered in relationships with black men often accused the black men of assault. In cases where the women did not make this accusation, white men would make it for them since they wanted to maintain their own reputations in the community.

Wells was in Philadelphia at a church convention when her editorial was published, and she was initially unaware of the **backlash** it caused. Edward Carmack, the editor of the *Memphis Commercial*, reprinted the editorial in his paper and threatened its author:

> The fact that a black scoundrel is allowed to live and utter such loathsome and repulsive calumnies is ... evidence as to the wonderful patience of Southern whites. But we have had enough of it. There are some things that the Southern white man will not tolerate.

Another white paper, the *Evening Scimitar*, openly advocated lynching: "Tie the wretch who utters these calumnies to a stake at the intersection of Main and Madison Sts., brand him in the forehead with a hot iron and perform upon him a surgical operation with a pair of tailor's shears."

Carmack and other leading white citizens formed a committee to deal with the problem. They destroyed the *Free Speech* office and searched for its owners. Fleming had already left the city, but Nightingale was found, beaten, and forced at gunpoint to sign a statement opposing the editorial. When Nightingale informed them that Wells had written the editorial, the committee posted lookouts at her house and the train station. It was rumored that if she returned, she would be hanged in front of the courthouse.

Wells then traveled to New York, and by the time she got there, she was aware of the events in Memphis. When T. Thomas Fortune offered her a job at the *New York Age*, she accepted. She wrote in her autobiography, "Having lost my paper, had a price put on my life, and been made an exile from home for hinting at the truth, I felt that I owed it to myself and to my race to tell the whole truth now that I was where I could do so freely."

Spreading the Word

As a weekly columnist for the *Age*, Wells was able to reach a new and larger audience. On June 25, 1892, she published a full report of her findings under the pseudonym "Exiled," and thousands of copies of the paper were distributed throughout the country. Wells was determined to educate people outside the South, who she believed would support her cause if they knew the facts.

One of the people she convinced was Frederick Douglass, who told her that her article opened his eyes to the reality of lynching. Like many others, Douglass had believed the

A portrait of former slave Frederick Douglass, who played an important role in the abolitionist movement and became the nation's most influential black leader. Douglass credited Wells with opening his eyes to America's lynching problem.

Southern lies about sexual assaults and had accepted lynching as an unpleasant but acceptable punishment for a horrible crime. Wells's article was a "revelation" to him, and he became one of her most influential supporters.

Wells found a great deal of support in New York, especially from the women in the black communities of Harlem and Brooklyn. She needed money to publish her first pamphlet—a full-length report of her lynching research—and the city's women organized a fundraiser in her honor. On October 5, 1892, hundreds of people from around the Northeast gathered at New York's Lyric Hall to hear Wells speak.

This was the most important speaking engagement Wells had accepted, and she was uncharacteristically nervous. Many influential black leaders were in attendance, and she knew it was crucial to deliver her message clearly. Her speech went smoothly until she told the story of the Curve lynchings. Wells started crying at the podium and had to take a moment to gather herself. She felt that she had failed and was disappointed in herself for breaking down, but her emotional display deeply moved the audience. She was presented with a gold brooch and $500, which she used to publish her first pamphlet, *Southern Horrors* (1892).

Spectacle Lynching

The publication of the first full-length study of lynching in America and her lecture tour throughout the Northeast made Wells the face of the growing anti-lynching movement. However, even though she had the ear of many influential activists, both black and white, lynchings were becoming more common and more brutal.

In February 1893, a black man named Henry Smith was lynched for the sexual assault and murder of a four-year-old girl in Paris, Texas. Myrtle Vance was the daughter of a former Paris policeman, and even though there was no evidence that the child had been assaulted, Vance claimed that she was. Smith was considered a "harmless, weak-minded" man, but he had been arrested and beaten by Vance in the past, and it was thought that he must have killed the child as revenge. The white community and press "exaggerate[d] every detail" and "inflame[d] the public mind so that nothing less than immediate and violent death would satisfy the populace."

Smith fled to Arkansas but he was captured and returned to Texas by train. His lynching was advertised ahead of time, and there were special trains that ran to Paris specifically to take people to the event. Ten thousand people—including women and children—gathered to watch what was known as a spectacle lynching. The *New York Sun* reported the gory details: Smith "was placed upon a carnival float in mockery of

This 1893 photograph shows the spectacle lynching of Henry Smith in Paris, Texas. Ten thousand people were in Paris to watch the murder of Smith, who is tied up on a scaffold with the word "Justice" written on it.

Ida B. Wells-Barnett and the Crusade against Lynching

a king upon his throne" and "escorted through the city so that all might see the inhuman monster." He was "placed upon a scaffold … within the view of all beholders" and "tortured for fifty minutes by red-hot iron brands," then "kerosene was poured upon him" and his body was burned. Spectators fought for pieces of charred bone and teeth to take as souvenirs, but still the mob was not satisfied. They found Smith's stepson, William Butler, and hanged him even though he had committed no crime.

News of this atrocity spread across the Atlantic and was particularly disturbing to English activist Catherine Impey. She had heard Wells speak in Philadelphia and was so horrified by the Paris lynchings that she and fellow activist Isabelle Mayo invited Wells to Britain for a lecture tour. To Wells, this invitation was "like an open door in a stone wall" since her work at home was not having enough of an impact. The white press was silent in the North and hostile in the South, and the federal government, fearing another civil war, was unwilling to pass any anti-lynching laws. British opinion had been influential during the abolitionist movement, so Wells sailed for England, hoping that the same would be true for her cause.

A Crusader for Justice

I da B. Wells's travels abroad brought the horrors of lynching to the world's attention and allowed her to make more of an impact at home. However, her aggressive, unapologetic style and her willingness to tell the hard truth about race relations in America made her a lot of new enemies. Controversy seemed to follow Wells wherever she went, but she did not let that stop her from doing the work she felt was her calling.

Transatlantic Activism

Like many in the United States, the British believed the South's lies about black men. They also believed that lynching was a form of **frontier justice**—a way to punish criminals in areas where there were no organized lawmen or courts. Wells hoped that by speaking the truth, she could show them that lynching was actually an illegal form of racial violence that stripped black Americans of their rights to a trial and protection under the law. She also believed that by reporting the facts, including cases where women and children were lynched, she could disprove the South's claim that lynching was a punishment reserved for black men who sexually assaulted white women.

During her six-week trip in 1893, Wells averaged a lecture a day. She traveled across England and Scotland, helping Impey and Mayo organize local chapters of the Society for Recognition of the Universal Brotherhood of Man (SRUBM). Wells gave lectures to members who then signed anti-lynching resolutions and petitions to the American government. Her travels were reported extensively in the British press.

Press coverage was mostly positive, but there were some naysayers. A city councilman wrote a letter to the *Birmingham Daily Post*, questioning the purpose of Wells's visit. He wrote, "I protest against being expected to give my attention to matters of municipal detail in a civilized country at a great distance," and he felt it would be "an impertinence" for the English to interfere with American matters. Wells responded with her own letter, stating that the anti-lynching movement needed help from the British people, who "did much for the final overthrow of chattel slavery ... America cannot and will not ignore the voice of a nation that is her superior in civilization, which makes this demand in the name of justice and humanity."

Wells returned to Britain for a second tour in 1894, this time as the first black foreign correspondent for a white paper, the *Chicago Inter-Ocean*. It was a huge milestone for Wells to have the support of a white paper. She was paid for a weekly column, "Ida B. Wells Abroad," in which she could detail the events of her lecture tour for white readers. Her second trip was successful, but fraught with controversy.

Wells got caught in the middle of a petty feud between Impey and Mayo. When Wells refused to take sides, she was

A photograph of the 1911 lynching of a woman, Laura Nelson, and her son, Lawrence. Wells used the fact that women and children were lynched to debunk the Southern rationalization for lynching as punishment for sexual assault.

left without the support and funding of the SRUBM. She did not let this stop her, and she continued on her tour with the help of Reverend Charles Aked, a Liverpool pastor who helped her get speaking engagements and press coverage. The British Parliament held a dinner in her honor in London, and she met with many of the city's elite editors, ministers, lords, and ladies. By the end of her tour, a group of London's most influential citizens formed the British Anti-Lynching Committee, dedicated to raising money and awareness for her cause.

Despite all the support Wells had gathered on her tour, the American government failed to pass any anti-lynching laws. George H. White, the only black House representative, followed Wells's work and introduced an anti-lynching bill in Congress in 1900, but it was defeated. With no help from the government, these crimes still went unpunished, but Wells kept writing and investigating. She documented the lynchings of Sam Hose and Elijah Strickland in Palmetto, Georgia, in *Lynch Law in Georgia* (1899). There were also an increasing number of race riots in American cities. The July 1900 riot in New Orleans, Louisiana, was covered in her pamphlet *Mob Rule in New Orleans* (1900).

The July 28, 1900, edition of the New Orleans *Daily Picayune* reports on the death of Robert Charles and the subsequent race riot, which Wells covered in her pamphlet *Mob Rule in New Orleans*.

A Gruesome Invitation

In the summer of 1893, in between her two trips abroad, Wells settled in Chicago and began gathering material for another anti-lynching pamphlet, *A Red Record* (1895). Just weeks after her return, she received the following telegram at the *Inter-Ocean* office: "Lee Walker, colored man, accused of raping white women, in jail here, will be taken out and burned

Wells v. Washington

Ida B. Wells met with resistance not only with Southern whites. At the turn of the century, Booker T. Washington was the nation's most influential black leader. He was president of the Tuskegee Institute (which focused on industrial education) and was especially popular with whites because of his accommodationist approach to race relations. He answered a racist's disgusting accusation that black men lusted after white women by saying there were some black men who needed to be removed from black communities because they preyed on white women. Washington believed that technical education and self-improvement would lead to equality. In his "Atlanta Compromise" speech in 1895, he accepted segregation, stating that "in all things that are purely social, we can be as separate as the fingers, yet one as the hand in all things essential to mutual progress." He rejected activism as a means of racial uplift and called on black Americans to focus on the fields of manual labor:

> Our greatest danger is that in the great leap from slavery to freedom we may overlook the fact that the masses of us are to live by the productions of our hands … No race can prosper till it learns that there is as much dignity in tilling a field as in writing a poem. It is at the bottom of life we must begin, and not at the top.

Influential black leader Booker T. Washington (*middle right*) stands with white supporters (*left to right*) Robert C. Ogden, William Howard Taft, and Andrew Carnegie, on the steps of a building at Tuskegee Institute (now University), a historically black college in Alabama founded by Washington.

In her 1904 speech "Booker T. Washington and His Critics," Wells attacked Washington's head-in-the-sand approach to lynching and his motivations:

> Washington says in substance: Give me money to educate the Negro and when he is taught how to work, he will not commit the crime for which lynching is done ... [but he] knows when he says this that lynching is not invoked to punish crime but color ... The Negro ... knows by sad experience that industrial education will not [take the] place of political, civil, and intellectual liberty, and he objects to being deprived of fundamental rights of American citizenship to the end that [Tuskegee] shall flourish.

by whites to-night. Can you send Miss Ida Wells to write it up?" It was sent from the *Memphis Public Ledger* ten hours before the lynching occurred—proof that the lynching was both officially sanctioned and planned ahead of time.

The citizens of Memphis were influenced by newspaper descriptions of Walker. *The Appeal-Avalanche*, as quoted in the book *Lethal Punishment*, wrote this about him:

> The prisoner presented a loathsome spectacle. He is tall and slender, but the muscles stand out on his sinewy arms in bold relief. His face is a revolting mixture of cunning and bestiality. The eyes are small and dull, the nose broad and flat, and the lips are very full and prominent. On being asked for a story on his crimes, Walker began a tale which, for unreasoning lust and brutality, stands unparalleled in the black annals of negro outrages.

Wells was not at the office to receive the telegram and she was unable to do anything to stop the lynching. On July 22, a mob dragged Walker from his jail cell, hung him from a telephone pole in the center of the city, and mutilated and burned his body in front of a crowd of spectators. Per usual, the assault allegations were false. Walker's probable crime was frightening two white women who were driving a wagon by demanding something to eat.

Southern Sabotage

Wells's success abroad infuriated Southerners, and the papers tried to slander and discredit her. The May 26, 1894, edition of the *Memphis Commercial* attacked her character, calling her a "notorious courtesan" and accusing her of being the "paramour" of her former partner, Reverend Nightingale. They even included a quote from a black man, J. Thomas Turner, who stated, "All informed colored people know that the statements which Ida Wells is making in her addresses in England are false and slanderous." The *Commercial* was so desperate to thwart Wells's progress that they hired a black man, J. W. A. Shaw, and sent him to England to give speeches contradicting Wells's claims. Shaw told British audiences that "the Negro was not deprived of his vote and when lynched deserved it for terrible crimes."

British clergymen often asked Wells what their American counterparts were doing to help the cause. In one of her *Inter-Ocean* dispatches, Wells reported the answer she always gave: "they are too busy saving the souls of white Christians from future burning in hell-fire to save the lives of black ones from present burning in flames kindled by white Christians." Wells was not afraid to criticize American churches that remained silent on lynching. She told her audiences about segregation in Southern churches and accused the Northern clergy of ignoring the problem in order to maintain peace with their Southern congregations.

The British were troubled by the inaction of American churches and many published open letters to American congregations. After hearing Wells lecture at the Hope Street Church in Liverpool, Reverend Richard Acland Armstrong penned a letter to the *Christian Register*, a Boston Unitarian paper. Boston had been at the center of abolitionist activity before the Civil War, and Armstrong expressed his "great disturbance of soul" in learning that Boston Christians were "passive in the face of sickening brutalities" and "silent when their fellow citizens are scourged and flayed and burnt without trial or appeal."

National Afro-American Council

In 1896, the US Supreme Court's verdict in *Plessy v. Ferguson* legalized racial segregation in America. As Wells had done years before, a Louisiana man named Homer Plessy refused

ANOTHER JIM CROW CAR CASE.

Arrest of a Negro Traveler Who Per-
sisted in Riding With the
White People.

On Tuesday evening a negro named
Adolph Plessy was arrested by Private
Detective Cain on the East Louisiana
train and locked up for violating section 2 of act 111 of 1890, relative to separate coaches.

It appears that Plessy purchased a
ticket to Covington, and shortly before
his arrest the conductor asked him if
he was a colored man. On the latter
replying that he was the conductor informed him that he would have to g-
into the car set aside for colored peopl
This he refused to do, and Mr. Ca
then stepped up and requested him
go into the other coach, but he still re
fused, and Mr. Cain thereupon informed him that he would either have
to go or go to jail. He replied that he
would sooner go to jail than leave the
coach, and was thereupon arrested.

He waived examination yesterday
before Recorder Moulin, and was sent
before the criminal court under $500
bonds.

This clipping from the June 9, 1892, issue of the New Orleans *Daily Picayune* reports the arrest of Homer Plessy for violating Jim Crow train car laws. The case went to the Supreme Court, which ruled that "separate but equal" facilities were legal.

to sit in a Jim Crow train car in 1892. His case went to the highest court in the land, which ruled that "separate but equal" segregation in public transportation and other facilities did not violate the Constitution. This verdict reinforced the idea that blacks were inferior to whites, and it increased racial violence that fueled the civil rights movement well into the twentieth century.

The Plessy decision stripped black Americans of their civil rights, and lynchings continued unchecked. Prompted by the 1898 lynching of South Carolina postmaster Frazier B. Baker, T. Thomas Fortune and Bishop Alexander Waters called for a conference of black leaders to organize a new civil rights organization, the National Afro-American Council (NAAC).

Fortune invited Wells to the Rochester, New York, meeting in September and she became one of the founding members.

The NAAC called an emergency meeting in Washington, DC, late in 1898, after a bloody race riot in Wilmington, North Carolina. Wells and other delegates met with President William McKinley and lobbied for federal anti-lynching laws. McKinley had not responded to the lynching of Baker (a federal employee) or the Wilmington riot. At the meeting, Wells gave a speech, "Mob Violence and Anarchy," in which she criticized McKinley for his silence and inaction. She told the crowd, "We have at last come to the point in our race history where we must do something for ourselves and do it now."

Wells was elected financial secretary of the NAAC, to the dismay of many male members. There was a lot of opposition to Wells being in a position of leadership within the organization because she was considered too radical, and some men used sexist arguments to oppose her. The *Colored American* called her election an "unfortunate incident" and flat-out stated that "the financial secretary of the [NAAC] should be a man." Wells served as secretary for a year before resigning to organize and chair the NAAC's anti-lynching bureau.

The Birth of the NAACP

In August 1908, racial violence moved to the North. During a riot in Springfield, Illinois, white mobs destroyed black businesses and homes, and "three Negroes were lynched under the shadow of Abraham Lincoln's tomb." This event brought together white and black reformers, including Wells, who issued "The Call" to action. The National Negro Conference in Spring 1909 established a new organization: the National Association for the Advancement of Colored People (NAACP).

At the meeting, Wells gave a speech, "Lynching, Our National Crime," in which she stated three facts: "First:

W. E. B. Du Bois, founding member of the NAACP, is pictured in this 1918 photograph. Even though Wells was instrumental in the establishment of the NAACP, she was left off the "Founding Forty" members list because she was a controversial figure.

Lynching is color line murder. Second: Crimes against women is the excuse, not the cause. Third: It is a national crime and requires a national remedy." She called for federal anti-lynching laws and asked the conference to establish its own anti-lynching bureau "for the investigation and publication of the details of every lynching."

The NAACP ultimately took up anti-lynching work, but despite her lifelong contributions to the cause, Wells was left off the "Founding Forty" list of members. The list was dominated by white reformers, with only a small group of black leaders included. Again, she was considered too controversial to lead. Wells had very little involvement with the organization from this point on, choosing instead to focus on matters affecting her new hometown of Chicago, Illinois.

Cairo Lynching

Due in part to Wells's efforts, Illinois passed a law in 1905 calling for the removal of any law enforcement officer who did not act to prevent lynching. The law was put to the test in 1909, when Frog James was lynched in Cairo, Illinois. In violation of the law, Sheriff Frank Davis failed to prevent the lynching and may even have taken part. Wells petitioned Governor Charles S. Deneen to remove Davis from office, which he did, but Davis was granted a hearing with Deneen in which he would likely be reinstated.

Initially, Wells did not think she was the right person to attend the hearing, since she was not a lawyer. Her family insisted, with her eldest child telling her, "Mother, if you don't go, nobody else will!" Wells agreed to go to Cairo and investigate so she could present the facts at Davis's hearing.

After interviewing residents of Cairo, she had enough evidence to present at Davis's hearing in Springfield. She told Governor Deneen, "If this man is reinstated, it will simply mean an increase in lynchings in the state of Illinois and an encouragement to mob violence." Deneen ruled against

Davis's reinstatement, stating that there was no room for lynch law (protection from prosecution for involvement in lynching) in Illinois. This was the only victory Wells ever achieved in her crusade for effective anti-lynching legislation.

Illinois governor Charles S. Deneen, pictured in a 1908 photograph, ruled against lynch laws after Frog James was lynched.

Unsung Hero

T hough Wells never abandoned her anti-lynching crusade, in her later years she began to focus on women's issues and local problems in Chicago, where she had settled with her husband and started a family.

Nineteenth-century women formed civic clubs as a way to influence their communities and effect change, since they could not yet vote or hold office. Many of the established women's clubs were for white women only and did not address the needs of the black community, especially when it came to combating lynching and racial discrimination. Wells played a key role in the black women's club movement that began in the late nineteenth century. In 1893, she founded Chicago's first black women's civic club, later named the Ida B. Wells Club in her honor. As president of the Ida B. Wells Club, she established the first kindergarten in Chicago's black community and lobbied against segregation in city schools.

Anti-lynching protestors from the National Association of Colored Women form a picket line next to the White House on July 30, 1946.

Wells was also a founding member of the first national black women's organization, the National Association of Colored Women (NACW). The NACW was formed in response to an 1895 letter written by John Jacks, president of the Missouri Press Association, in which he tried to discredit Wells's anti-lynching work abroad. Jacks wrote a public letter denouncing the black race and addressed it to British Anti-Lynching Committee secretary Florence Balgarnie. He wrote that the black race was "wholly devoid of morality" and that black women "were prostitutes … natural liars and thieves." This attack on black women's virtue did not go unanswered. The nation's leading black females gathered together to form the NACW in 1896. They adopted the motto "Lifting As We Climb" and campaigned for **women's suffrage** and anti-lynching legislation.

Even though Wells was integral to the beginning of the NACW, she was considered unfit for leadership because of her aggressive style and the fact that she opposed the influential Booker T. Washington. She was not even invited to the 1899 NACW meeting in Chicago. Wells considered this "a staggering blow and all the harder to understand because it was women whom I had started in club work, and to whom I had given all the assistance in my power."

Negro Fellowship League

Chicago's black population grew as Jim Crow laws became more restrictive in the South. Many migrants, most of them rural young black men, arrived in the city with no place to live and no job. Housing discrimination created the "Black Belt" along State Street on Chicago's South Side, where the only accommodations for poor black migrants were in saloons or gambling houses. Many men ended up in jail not long after arriving in the city. The YMCA and other community aid organizations were for whites only, and Wells attributed the rise in crime among black Chicagoans to the fact that "only

Marriage and Children

Wells met her husband, Ferdinand Barnett, in Chicago while she was working with Frederick Douglass on a pamphlet protesting the 1893 World's Columbian Exposition. Black leaders were disturbed that the organizers of the fair, which was dedicated to showcasing American achievements, had left out the contributions of black Americans. Douglass and Wells distributed *The Reason Why the Colored American Is Not in the Worlds' Columbian Exposition* from Haiti's pavilion.

Barnett was a lawyer, civil rights advocate, and founder of Chicago's first black newspaper, the *Conservator*. He offered Wells a reporting job, and two years later they were married. Always ahead of her time, she chose to hyphenate her name and became known as Ida B. Wells-Barnett. They would have four children: Charles Aked, Herman Kohlsaat, Ida Bell, and Alfreda.

Barnett was a good match for Wells. He respected her work and did not expect her just to stay home and raise their children. He always encouraged her and supported her. Although she slowed the pace of her anti-lynching work while her children were young, she was still deeply committed to her crusade.

one social center welcomes the Negro, and that is the saloon."

In 1910, Wells established the Negro Fellowship League (NFL) Reading Room and Social Center on State Street. The league provided new arrivals to Chicago with a safe space free of alcohol, gambling, and other vices. Visitors could read from the extensive library and attend Bible study and weekly lectures by prominent reformers and intellectuals. The league soon expanded to offer men's lodging for 50 cents a night and gave vouchers for food at a restaurant across the street. There was also an employment bureau that helped migrants find jobs. Wells's husband, Ferdinand Barnett, who was assistant state's attorney at the time, often sent young men to the center for job assistance.

The league did not have much funding, so Wells got a job as Chicago's first female adult probation officer. She used her salary to support the league, and she helped her probationers get work through the NFL employment bureau. Through the league, Wells and her husband helped represent many prisoners and secured the release of falsely convicted men.

Women's Suffrage

The women's suffrage movement (the fight for women's right to vote) was a major reform movement in the late nineteenth

White women march in a 1910 suffrage parade in New York City. Wells was active in the suffrage movement, creating controversy when she refused to march in a segregated section in the 1913 Washington, DC, suffrage parade.

and early twentieth centuries. Wells had always believed that political participation was the best way to effect change for her race and her gender, and she was politically active long before women had the vote nationally. In 1896, she toured Illinois with the Women's State Republican Committee, campaigning for candidates and giving political speeches with a six-month-old son in tow. Wells combined her civic duties and her maternal duties, and she believed that she was "the only woman in the United States who ever traveled throughout the country with a nursing baby to make political speeches."

There was a great deal of racism within the women's suffrage movement because many white women felt that excluding black women would help their cause. They needed the support of Southern women, and they appealed to them on the grounds that, by excluding black women, the white female vote would cancel out the black male vote in the South. The largest women's suffrage organization, the National American Woman Suffrage Association (NAWSA), discouraged black women from participating.

In the early twentieth century, Wells "saw that we were likely to have a restricted suffrage, and the white women of the organization were working like beavers to bring it about," so she founded her own organization in 1913. The Alpha Suffrage Club (ASC) was the first black woman's suffrage organization. Wells and other delegates from the ASC attended the first women's suffrage parade in Washington, DC, which was organized by the NAWSA. Wells refused to march in the segregated section at the back of the parade and joined the white women from the Illinois delegation.

With more than two hundred members, the ASC canvassed the neighborhoods and held weekly sessions to educate women on political issues. Illinois passed a law in 1914 allowing all women to vote in local elections, and the ASC registered thousands of women in Chicago's Second Ward. The women encountered a lot of resistance from black men, who "jeered at them and told them they should be home taking care of the babies" and accused them of "trying to take the place of men and wear the trousers." Even in the face of opposition from their own race, Wells and the others soldiered on so that they could help get a black man elected to the city council. Due

ADVERTISEMENT   ADVERTISEMENT   ADVERTISEMENT   ADVERTISEMENT

THE SHAME OF AMERICA

Do you know that the <u>United States</u> is the <u>Only Land on Earth</u> where human beings are <u>BURNED AT THE STAKE?</u>

In Four Years, 1918-1921, Twenty-Eight People Were Publicly BURNED BY AMERICAN MOBS

3436 People Lynched 1889 to 1922

For What Crimes Have Mobs Nullified Government and Inflicted the Death Penalty?

The Alleged Crimes	The Victims	Why Some Mob Victims Died:
Murder	1288	Not turning out of road for white boy in auto
Rape	571	Being a relative of a person who was lynched
Crimes against the Person	615	Jumping a labor contract
Crimes against Property	333	Being a member of the Non-Partisan League
Miscellaneous Crimes	453	"Talking back" to a white man
Absence of Crime	176	"Insulting" white man.
	3436	

Is Rape the "Cause" of Lynching?

Of 3,436 people murdered by mobs in our country, only 571, or less than 17 per cent., were even accused of the crime of rape.

83 WOMEN HAVE BEEN LYNCHED IN THE UNITED STATES

Do lynchers maintain that they were lynched for "the usual crime"?

AND THE LYNCHERS GO UNPUNISHED

THE REMEDY

The Dyer Anti-Lynching Bill Is Now Before the United States Senate

The Dyer Anti-Lynching Bill was passed on January 26, 1922, by a vote of 230 to 119 in the House of Representatives

The Dyer Anti-Lynching Bill Provides:
That culpable State officers and mobbists shall be tried in Federal Courts on failure of State courts to act, and that a county in which a lynching occurs shall be fined $10,000, recoverable in a Federal Court.

The Principal Question Raised Against the Bill is upon the Ground of Constitutionality.

The *Constitutionality* of the Dyer Bill Has Been Affirmed by
The Judiciary Committee of the House of Representatives
The Judiciary Committee of the Senate
The United States Attorney General, legal adviser of Congress
Judge Guy D. Goff, of the Department of Justice

The Senate has been petitioned to pass the Dyer Bill by
29 Lawyers and Jurists, including two former Attorneys General of the United States
19 State Supreme Court Justices
24 State Governors
3 Archbishops, 85 bishops and prominent churchmen
39 Mayors of large cities, north and south.

The American Bar Association at its meeting in San Francisco, August 9, 1922, adopted a resolution asking for further legislation by Congress to punish and prevent lynching and mob violence.

Fifteen State Conventions of 1922—3 of them Democratic—have inserted in their party platforms a demand for national action to stamp out lynchings.

The Dyer Anti-Lynching Bill is not intended to protect the guilty, but to assure to every person accused of crime trial by due process of law.

THE DYER ANTI-LYNCHING BILL IS NOW BEFORE THE SENATE
TELEGRAPH YOUR SENATORS TODAY YOU WANT IT ENACTED

If you want to help the organization which has brought to light the facts about lynching, the organization which is fighting for 100 per cent. Americanism, not for some of the people some of the time, but for all of the people, white or black, all of the time

Send your check to J. E. SPINGARN, Treasurer of the

NATIONAL ASSOCIATION FOR THE ADVANCEMENT OF COLORED PEOPLE
70 FIFTH AVENUE, NEW YORK CITY

THIS ADVERTISEMENT IS PAID FOR IN PART BY THE ANTI-LYNCHING CRUSADERS.

This 1922 NAACP handbill promotes awareness of the Dyer Anti-Lynching Bill, which would have made lynching a federal crime. It failed to pass, and the US government never enacted any specific anti-lynching legislation.

in large part to the Alpha Suffrage Club's influence, Oscar DePriest was elected Chicago's first black **alderman** in 1915.

The Nineteenth Amendment granting woman the right to vote was ratified in 1920. In 1930, Wells became one of the first black women to run for public office when she campaigned as an independent for an Illinois state senate seat. She knew she did not have nearly enough funds or support to win, but she ran anyway because she was disillusioned by the nominees of the major political parties.

Return to the South

After nearly thirty years in exile, Wells returned to the South to interview twelve death-row inmates in Helena, Arkansas. The black men were arrested and sentenced to death after a riot in Elaine, Arkansas, in which hundreds of black people were murdered. The riot started at a meeting of the Progressive Farmers and Household Union on September 30, 1919, which was organized by **sharecroppers** who wanted to get fair prices for their cotton crops. White landowners often took advantage of black farmers under the sharecropping system, and the white landowners saw this group as a threat.

A group of armed white men came to the church where the meeting was being held and a gunfight broke out in which a white man was killed. The white community claimed that the black men were organizing an uprising, and for three days after the shooting, white posses patrolled the region, killing innocent black citizens. The governor of Arkansas sanctioned the violence and even sent in troops to put down the supposed insurrection.

Wells went to the prison where the twelve inmates were being held, posing as a family member to disguise herself since she was still not safe in the South. She interviewed all the men and found that "the terrible crime these men had committed was to organize their members into a union for the purpose of getting the market price for their cotton …

[and] get out from under the white landlord's thumb." She published her findings, including her interviews with the inmates and the court proceedings from their trials, in *The Arkansas Race Riot* (1920). Although the NAACP handled the legal work involved in the case, Wells's visit brought hope to the men, who were acquitted and released in 1923.

Ida B. Wells died of **uremia** on March 25, 1931. She almost single-handedly brought America's lynching problem to the world's attention, but history did not fully recognized her achievements until long after her death. Her insistence on telling the ugly truth, regardless of whom she offended, and her unwillingness to compromise on the issues she held dear made her a controversial figure. She was pushed into the background when other organizations began to take up her cause. It was not until much later, after the civil rights movement of the 1960s, when historians began to take note of her work. Wells was not given the recognition she deserved in her time, but she is considered by many to be the mother of the civil rights movement. Her trailblazing work set up later generations of activists to succeed in gaining the full legal rights that Wells knew her race deserved.

Chronology

Dates in green pertain to events discussed in this volume.

1862 Ida Bell Wells is born on July 16 in Holly Springs, Mississippi.

1863 The Emancipation Proclamation is issued by President Abraham Lincoln.

1865 The Thirteenth Amendment, abolishing slavery, is passed in the US House of Representatives. The amendment was passed by the Senate in 1864.

1866 Radical Reconstruction begins; Congress passes the Civil Rights Act over President Andrew Johnson's veto, granting full civil rights and citizenship to all people born in the US regardless of race or former slave status; the Ku Klux Klan is formed in Tennessee.

1867 Congress passes the Reconstruction Act over Johnson's veto, placing the Southern states under military control.

1868 The Fourteenth Amendment, guaranteeing equal rights under the law, is passed.

1870 The Fifteenth Amendment, prohibiting governments from denying male citizens the right to vote based on their race, is passed.

1875 The Civil Rights Act of 1875 gives equal rights to black people in public places, public transportation, and jury service.

1883 The Supreme Court strikes down the Civil Rights Act of 1875. Ida B. Wells is forcibly removed from a train when she refuses to move from the ladies' car to the "colored" car.

1884 Wells sues the railroad and wins; she writes her first article for the *Living Way*. The verdict in the railroad lawsuit is overturned by the Tennessee Supreme Court in 1887.

1892 The March 9 lynchings in Memphis begin Wells's lifelong crusade; Wells writes a May 21 editorial that results in destruction of the *Free Speech* newspaper and her exile from the South.

1896 *Plessy v. Ferguson*, establishing the precedent of "separate but equal," is handed down by the Supreme Court of the United States.

1900 In a fourteen-year period ending at the turn of the century, more than 2,500 African Americans are lynched, most in the Deep South.

1909 The National Association for the Advancement of Colored People (NAACP) is established with Ida B. Wells as a founding member. Wells successfully fights to enforce an Illinois anti–mob violence law after the lynching of Frog James in Cairo, IL.

1913 Ida B. Wells founds the Alpha Suffrage Club; she marches alongside white women in a Washington, DC, suffrage parade and meets with President Woodrow Wilson regarding segregation of federal employees.

1931 Ida B. Wells dies of uremia (kidney disease) in Chicago on March 25.

1935 Thurgood Marshall and Charles Hamilton Houston successfully sue the University of Maryland, arguing for Donald Murray's admission to the institution's law school in *Murray v. Pearson*. The two argue that as the state does not provide a public law school for African Americans, it does not provide adequate "separate but equal" institutions.

1941 President Franklin D. Roosevelt bans discrimination against minorities in the granting of defense contracts.

1947 Jackie Robinson breaks the color barrier in Major League Baseball.

1954 Thurgood Marshall and the NAACP win the case of *Brown v. Board of Education of Topeka*, which overturns *Plessy v. Ferguson* and the "separate but equal" doctrine of segregation in the United States.

1955 Rosa Parks refuses to give up her seat to a white person on a bus in Montgomery, Alabama. Her arrest sparks a bus boycott that leads to buses being desegregated in that city.

1957 Federal troops are called in to protect nine African-American students in Little Rock, Arkansas, who are trying to attend all-white Central High School.

1961 Congress on Racial Equality organizes Freedom Rides throughout the South, and the riders suffer beatings from mobs in many cities.

1963 The March on Washington attracts a quarter of a million people, who listen to Martin Luther King Jr.'s "I Have a Dream" speech.

1964 President Lyndon B. Johnson signs the Civil Rights Act of 1964. It prohibits discrimination of all kinds.

1965 Congress passes the Voting Rights Act, which guarantees to all African Americans the right to vote.

1967 The Supreme Court rules that laws prohibiting interracial marriage are unconstitutional.

2003 The Supreme Court upholds a policy at the University of Michigan Law School, ruling that race can be used as a consideration in admitting students.

Glossary

alderman A member of the municipal legislative body in a town or city.

anti-miscegenation laws Laws that criminalized interracial marriage and consensual relationships between members of different races.

backlash A strong reaction by a large group of people, especially to social or political change.

black codes Laws enacted by Southern states after the Civil War to restrict the rights of ex-slaves, maintain white supremacy, and ensure the continued supply of cheap labor.

blackface Dark face paint applied by a white person in an attempt to make them appear black.

consensual relationships Relationships that are mutually agreed upon by both persons, and in which both persons are free to make that choice.

disenfranchise To prevent a person or group (e.g., black Americans) from exercising their legal right to vote.

frontier justice An extralegal form of punishment for criminals in areas where there is no organized justice system.

Jim Crow laws Laws that deprived black Americans of their civil rights and legalized racial discrimination and segregation.

literacy test An exam taken to determine if a person can read and write well enough to qualify to vote. These tests were used in the South to prevent uneducated black Americans and recent immigrants from voting. Literacy tests were outlawed by the Voting Rights Act of 1965.

lynching The mob murder of an alleged criminal (commonly a black person) without a legal trial.

poll tax A tax that every adult must pay in order to vote, regardless of income. The tax was used to prevent poor people, especially blacks, from voting.

pseudonym A false name used by an author.

race man A member of the black community active in business as well as social and political groups dedicated to the uplift of the race.

sharecroppers People working in a system of agriculture in the post–Civil War South where a poor farmer, often black, raises crops for a white landowner and receives a portion of the value of the crop.

uremia A severe form of kidney disease.

Victorian-era Describing the time from 1837 to 1901 during which Queen Victoria reigned in Great Britain. Victorian society was ruled by strict standards of etiquette, especially in the relationship of unmarried people of the opposite sex.

women's suffrage A reform movement to secure women the right to vote in national elections.

yellow fever A life-threatening infectious disease spread by mosquitoes that causes severe liver and kidney damage.

Further Information

Books

Fradin, Dennis Brindell, and Judith Bloom Fradin.
Ida B. Wells: Mother of the Civil Rights Movement.
New York: Clarion Books, 2000.

Hinman, Bonnie. *Eternal Vigilance: The Story of Ida B.
Wells–Barnett*. Greensboro, NC: Morgan Reynolds, 2010.

Lisandrelli, Elaine Slivinski. *Ida B. Wells–Barnett: Crusader
against Lynching*. African-American Biographies. Berkeley
Heights, NJ: Enslow, 1998.

Uschan, Michael V. *Lynching and Murder in the Deep South*.
San Diego, CA: Lucent, 2006.

Wormser, Richard. *The Rise and Fall of Jim Crow*.
New York: St. Martin's Griffin, 2004.

Websites

**Civil Rights For Kids: African-American
Civil Rights Movement**
www.ducksters.com/history/civil_rights/african-american_
civil_rights_movement.php

This overview of the civil rights movement provides
information about events and links to stories on important
people who shaped those events.

The Mississippi Writers Page: Ida B. Wells-Barnett

mwp.olemiss.edu//dir/wells-barnett_ida/

The University of Mississippi biography of Ida B. Wells-Barnett comes with an extensive bibliography and links to other publications that cover her part in the civil rights movement.

PBS: The Rise and Fall of Jim Crow

www.pbs.org/wnet/jimcrow/index.html

The Public Broadcasting System has built a learning center that covers a wide range of topics relating to Jim Crow laws and racism, and even provides lesson plans for teachers.

Bibliography

Bay, Mia. *To Tell the Truth Freely: The Life of Ida B. Wells.* New York: Hill and Wang, 2009.

DeCosta-Willis, Miriam, ed. *The Memphis Diary of Ida B. Wells.* Boston: Beacon Press, 1995.

Dray, Philip. *At the Hands of Persons Unknown: The Lynching of Black America.* New York: Modern Library, 2003.

Duster, Alfreda M., ed. *Crusader For Justice: The Autobiography of Ida B. Wells.* Chicago: University of Chicago Press, 1970.

Fradin, Dennis Brindell, and Judith Bloom Fradin. *Ida B. Wells: Mother of the Civil Rights Movement.* New York: Clarion Books, 2000.

Giddings, Paula J. *Ida: A Sword Among Lions.* New York: HarperCollins, 2008.

Hinman, Bonnie. *Eternal Vigilance: The Story of Ida B. Wells-Barnett.* Greensboro, NC: Morgan Reynolds, 2010.

Lisandrelli, Elaine Slivinski. *Ida B. Wells-Barnett: Crusader against Lynching.* African-American Biographies. Berkeley Heights, NJ: Enslow, 1998.

McMurray, Linda. *To Keep the Waters Troubled: The Life of Ida B. Wells.* New York: Oxford University Press, 1998.

Royster, Jacqueline Jones, ed. *Southern Horrors and Other Writings: The Anti-Lynching Campaign of Ida B. Wells, 1892–1900.* Boston: Bedford/St. Martin's, 1997.

Schechter, Patricia A. *Ida B. Wells-Barnett and American Reform, 1880–1930*. Chapel Hill, NC: University of North Carolina Press, 2001.

Silkey, Sarah L. *Black Woman Reformer: Ida B. Wells, Lynching, and Transatlantic Activism*. Athens, GA: University of Georgia Press, 2015.

Sterling, Dorothy. *Black Foremothers: Three Lives*. New York: The Feminist Press at CUNY, 1993.

Wells, Ida. B. *The Light of Truth: Writings of an Anti-Lynching Crusader*. Edited by Mia Bay. New York: Penguin Books, 2014.

———. "Lynching, Our National Crime." *Proceedings of the National Negro Conference 1909: New York, May 31 and June 1*. https://archive.org/details/procnatnegrocon00newyrich.

Index

Page numbers in **boldface** are illustrations. Entries in **boldface** are glossary terms.

alderman, 52
Alpha Suffrage Club, 50, 52
anti-miscegenation laws, 26

backlash, 26
Barnett, Ferdinand, 44, 47–48
black codes, 5, **5**
blackface, 25

Chicago, 35, 42, 44, 46–48, 50, 52
consensual relationships, 25–26
Curve, the, 20–25, **21**, 29

disenfranchise, **6**, 8
Douglass, Frederick, 17, 27, **28**, 47

Fortune, T. Thomas, 17, **17**, 27, 40–41
Freedmen's Bureau, 9–10, **10**, **19**, **22**
Free Speech, 18–19, 25, 27
frontier justice, 32

Jim Crow laws, 12, **13**, 40, **40**, 46

Ku Klux Klan, 9, **9**

literacy test, 8
Living Way, 15–16, 18
lynching
  Baker, Frazier B., 40–41
  Curve lynchings, 20–25, **21**, 29
  emergence of, 6
  James, Frog, 42–43, **43**
  legislation against, 34, 41–43, **43**, 46, **51**
  newspaper support of, **23**, 25, 27, 38–39
  sexual assault and, 23, 25–26, 29–30, 32–33, **34**, 37–39, 42
  Smith, Henry, 29–31, **30**

Memphis, 11–12, 14, 16, 18–22, **21**, **22**, 24, 26–27, 38

NAACP, 23, 41–42, **42**, **51**, 53
National Afro-American Council, 40

National Association of Colored Women, **45**, 46
Negro Fellowship League, 48
New York Age, 17, **17**, 27

Plessy v. Ferguson, 39–40, **40**
poll tax, 8
pseudonym, 16, 27

race man, 10
Reconstruction, 4–6, 8–9, **19**
riots, 20, **22**, 35, **35**, 41,52–53
Rust College, 10, **10**

segregation, 12, **13**, 36, 39–40, 44, **49**, 50
sharecroppers, 52

uremia, 53

Victorian-era, 16

Washington, Booker T., 36–37, **37**, 46
Wells-Barnett, Ida B.
    accessibility of writing, 18–19
    British tours, 31–34, 38–39
    childhood, 6–12
    early journalism career, 14–18, **14**

Free Speech and, 18–20, 24–27
lynching and, 23, 25–27, **28**, 29, 31–35, **34**, 37–39, 41–44, 46–47, 53
marriage, 47
other activism, 44, 48–50, **49**, 52
pamphlets, 29, 35, 47
pseudonyms, **14**, 16–17, 27
railroad segregation lawsuit, 12–14, 16
speeches, 28, 31–34, 37, 39, 41–42, 50
teaching, 12, 16, 19–20, **19**
women's suffrage, 46, 48–50, **49**

yellow fever, 11

About the Author

ALISON MORRETTA holds a bachelor of arts in English and creative writing from Kenyon College in Gambier, Ohio, where she studied literature and American history. She has written many nonfiction titles for middle and high school students on subjects such as the abolitionist movement, American literature, and Internet safety. She lives in New York City with her loving husband, Bart, and their rambunctious corgi, Cassidy.